poetry
Healing for the soul

by Kathleen Schubitz

Volume 1

Updated October 2024

POETRY: Healing for the soul
Volume 1
by Kathleen Schubitz

Published by:
RPJ & COMPANY, INC.
RPJandco.com
Orlando, Florida, U.S.A.

ISBN-13: 978-1-937770-58-7

Cover and Interior Design: Kathleen Schubitz

Cover Image by Kathleen Schubitz | Copyright © 2016-2024

Printed in the United States of America.

Table of Contents

Trapped or Free?

For many years I felt trapped,
    but now I'm free.
    Life choices once difficult
    now come with ease.

Growing up with peace
    in my background
    Was a rare occurrence;
    hostility was all around.

When I was wronged,
    I used to feel bitter.
    Now I choose to allow circumstances
    to make me better.

The enemy's plan has been
    one of leading me astray,
    With temptation and lies disguised
    by a beautiful array.

Playing or pretending to have
    the role of divinity,
    Vengeful feelings arose
    for every wrongdoer I called an enemy.

The choice to hate was easy,
    but I tried to choose love.
    The best choice always comes
    from the Father above.

Unknowingly I took on offense;
    it continued to grow.
    Back then I did not know
    I could be wiser for letting it go.

I used to hold onto hurt
    and emotional injury,
    But now I choose
    to let every prisoner go free!

Romans 12:19 - ...but rather give place unto wrath: for it is written, Vengeance is mine; I will repay, saith the Lord.

My True Identity

Years of lies planted
    by the enemy
    Identified me
    in what I believed.

Heavy chains
    had me bound;
    I felt as if
    I'd never get free.

Long ago
    soon after I was born,
    Hopeless and helpless
    is what I believed.

God's Word of truth
    came to set me free,
    But enemy lies
    were easier to believe.

His gentle ways
    of changing my mind
    Set me on a path
    to eternity.

He's changed my thinking
in what I believe,
With His songs of love
that He sings over me.

I've since surrendered
and opened my heart to believe,
To live in truth,
no longer deceived.

Jesus paid the price
to give me full liberty.
Now I can believe
and live my true identity.

Isaiah 61:1 - The Spirit of the Lord God is upon me; because the Lord hath anointed me to preach good tidings unto the meek; he hath sent me to bind up the brokenhearted, to proclaim liberty to the captives, and the opening of the prison to them that are bound;

I Am Free!

As I mature
    by God's loving hand,
    I seek deliverance
    to enter His promised land.

I choose to release anger
    I feel toward myself;
    I choose to stop drinking poison
    and hurting myself.

I release constant
    and nagging frustration
    And choose to be filled up
    at God's Love station.

Man was unable to meet
    my every need,
    But as I release anger,
    God's plants a loving seed.

Anxiety and depression
    come in like a flood.
    But with His stripes,
    I'm able to find healing and love.

Life choices
  can drudge up insecurity,
  But God promises
  to meet every need.

Feelings of bitterness
  from guilt and shame
  Are all washed away;
  I'm no longer the same.

Forgiveness for negative words
  and spirits sown
  Come as I repent from sin,
  rather than what I've known.

When emotions
  seem to flood my soul,
  I reflect on the Word;
  it tells me I'm whole.

Anger was so well disguised
  by God's enemy;
  Blinders kept me in bondage,
  but now I am free!

Galatians 5:1 - Stand fast therefore in the liberty wherewith Christ hath made us free, and be not entangled again with the yoke of bondage.

Forgive Me, Father

Anger became a way of life
    that once held me captive,
    But I determined to be happy,
    so unknowingly I disguised it.
    Satan wanted me to believe
    that I conquered the angry spirit,
    But the Lord revealed the open door
    so I could repent from it.

Once I agreed with the enemy
    by giving him an open invitation,
    His plan was that I would fail to dwell
    in God's holy habitation.
    Little did I know
    that spewing and stuffing every feeling
    Would cause such distress
    and heartache unreeling.

As I surrendered and sought Truth
    through the Holy Spirit,
    He revealed faith was overtaken by fear,
    He was no longer part of it.
    I was grieving and repenting
    for opening a door to the enemy;
    My soul needed release;
    wholeness failed to come quickly.

The Lord's spiritual eraser
won't undo the pain I've caused.
But I can take a few days
to reflect on my sin and pause…
"Forgive me Father
for against You I have truly sinned,
I repent and seek Your forgiveness;
make me whole again."

All the years that have been stolen
through believing I conquered anger;
My mind is now made up
to give You my feelings
and steer clear of danger.
No longer do I want to engage
in enemy tricks and messes;
Restore me to You,
loving and pleasing You
through any distresses.

Jeremiah 31:34 - …for I will forgive their iniquity,
and I will remember their sin no more.

Yielded to Truth

Be not deceived;
    understand the enemy's goal;
    It is to confuse and scatter
    every human soul.

He wants us to think
    we're free and already whole.
    And when we believe his lies,
    he's reached his goal.

Though satan is known
    as the prince of the air,
    We have the power to choose
    every word with care.

We must give the Lord all doubt,
    insecurity and fear,
    He desires relationship with us;
    He wants to be near.

God created us
    to be His hands and His feet,
    Share the good news
    to conquer feelings of defeat.

Yield emotions to the Lord
   rather than please the enemy.
The Holy Spirits leads us
   to find freedom and victory.

Healing and wholeness for us
   will eventually come
As we seek liberty and truth
   through God's only Son.

Galatians 6:7 - Be not deceived; God is not
mocked; for whatsoever a man soweth, that
shall he also reap.

Look Up!

When anger rises in me,
   I have a choice to spew or let it be.
   Or, it can be diffused
   by the One living inside of me.

It serves me
   when my life is at stake,
   But fuming or spewing
   can lead to a mistake.

If I take time to evaluate
   the emotion and behavior,
   The answers can be found
   through our loving Savior.

Will it help or hinder me
   by verbally expressing,
   Or cause the enemy to rob me
   of peace and blessing?

His plans for love and peace
   in every relationship
   Will outlast momentary fuming
   and future hardship.

The enemy wants me to stew,
   fume and blow up,
   But God desires yielding,
   so I must look up!

Thank You

When I allow emotions
    to get the best of me,
    It displeases the Lord,
    but pleases the enemy.

The Lord is eager to deliver me
    from anger and wrath;
    He is able to set my feet
    on a godly path.

The path that leads
    to peace and redemption.
    As I walk with Him,
    there's no more tension.

Surrendering to Him,
    I have peace
    Because in Him,
    emotions will cease.

So, here's my prayer:
    Lord, deliver me, defrag my soul,
    Only You can take the mess
    and make me whole.
    Bind me to love and the Spirit of truth;
    Walk me through the pain from youth.
    Thank you for loving and setting me free.
    Thank you for saving my soul
    and dying just for me!

Last Days

Satan tries to keep us
    depressed and miserable,
    But God's plan is not fiction,
    but biblical.

The Bible stories reveal
    the truth about Jesus;
    He overcame sin;
    He paid the price for us.

Jesus felt bitter, resentful,
    betrayal and shame;
    He felt everything,
    so we'd refuse the enemy's game.

The Lord died
    for the sins of all mankind,
    And the enemy failed
    for any sin to find.

He attempts to blind us
    with cloth like drape.
    God's love and truth
    always provide an escape.

The devil looks for open doors
in which he might succeed;
Believers choosing freedom
will be free indeed.

The enemy tempts us
in so many ways,
But we must be wise
in these last days.

1 Corinthians 10:13 - ...but will with the temptation also make a way to escape, that ye may be able to bear it.

Never Alone!

Am I secure in God's goodness,
   love and sovereignty?
   Am I content to live a life
   only for Him to please?

When insecurity rises,
   am I quick to feel anger or rage?
   When I know I'm loved,
   emotions quickly fade.

Can I seek peace
   rather than start a commotion?
   Can I feel what's truly
   lying beneath the emotion?

Emotional energies
   trigger something within;
   He will use them
   to draw me closer to Him.

The Holy Spirit comforts me
   with His love and embrace;
   I'm called to be kind
   and look for Jesus on each face.

I trust in the Holy Spirit
  and surrender every feeling,
  My heart feels more connected to Him:
  I find myself kneeling.

I am living under grace,
  ever before His throne.
  He filled me up with His Spirit,
  so I'm never alone!

*Psalm 62:1 - Truly my soul waiteth upon God:
from him cometh my salvation.*

Anger No More

While attending a local bible study
    the topic of anger was assigned.
    Up to this point,
    I failed to recognize
    that unresolved anger
    remained in me,
    within me it lied.

Satan tricked me into believing
    I was free through forgiving those
    who brought harm and injury.
    But processing anger
    was unknown to me,
    nor did I understand
    the Word personally.

I was broken and devastated
    deep down inside,
    for the sin of harboring anger,
    I could no longer hide.
    God's Word warns us
    against the sin of anger,
    To give the enemy no place,
    I refused its danger.

It hurt me to know
   I had sinned against my Lord,
   But His love for me reached out
   with His holy Word.
   Upon reflection and sorrow
   for more than a day,
   It's been dancing with me since
   before my first birthday.

The dance with anger
   I will dance no more;
   The Lord's truth will redeem,
   heal and restore.
   With the sin revealed
   and now recognized,
   It's time for indwelling anger
   to shrivel up and die!

Ephesians 4:26-27 - Be ye angry, and sin not: let not the sun go down upon your wrath: Neither give place to the devil.

The Life He Planned

Emotions can be strong for those
   who were unable to express.
   Feelings of anger and frustration
   and blame are always a mess.
   Jealousy might be felt
   when comparing ourselves to another,
   God created them to be a father,
   sister, brother or mother.

So we might argue
   and put up a fuss;
   He answers a prayer,
   someone's sent to help us.
   We often dislike
   who He sends our way,
   But He knows best,
   we're smart to obey.

When we feel tricked or trapped
   by a deceiving brother,
   It's best to surrender to Jesus,
   our only true brother.
   And when people steal,
   cheat or lie,
   It's up to us
   to look deeply inside.

Feelings of anger attract only negativity.
　　Rarely will anger meet any true need.
　　Poor choices lead us
　　along a downward path.
　　For our benefit,
　　God created the straight
　　and narrow path.

The blessed life for us
　　that He has planned
　　Is overflowing with goodness,
　　His promised land.
　　God's forgiveness and mercy
　　leads us to a life of love,
　　The life that He planned
　　from Heaven above.

Jeremiah 29:11 - For I know the thoughts that
I think toward you, saith the Lord, thoughts
of peace, and not of evil, to give you an
expected end.

Uncover It!

Stuffing it or denying it…
It's just another cover-up!

The enemy wants me to do it;
God's Word leads me to uncover it.

I'll uncover the truth hidden deeply inside
His Holy Spirit reveals truth and not lies:

The feelings of insecurity;
He knows exactly how I feel.

When peace is overtaken by worry and fear,
I can call on Him, His presence is near.

For depression, anger and hostility
He will calm the raging storm inside of me.

Denying and stuffing, I will do no more.
Jesus will uncover it, for He is my Lord!

John 8:32 - And ye shall know the truth, and the
truth shall make you free.

KATHLEEN SCHUBITZ is an accomplished author, poet, speaker and business woman. God's spoken word from Romans 14:17 birthed RPJ & Company (Righteousness, Peace and Joy) in 2004, thereby establishing a Kingdom publishing business for God's people. As founder and president, her faith in God and desire to follow His leading compels her to pursue her own writing and publish books, devotionals, poetry, calendars and marketing materials for leaders and Kingdom writers.

After growing up in the Midwestern United States, Kathleen presently resides in central Florida. Preparation for her calling comes from serving at Rotary International headquarters as production assistant for *The Rotarian* magazine. Having now become an inspirational writer, she lives a life of dedication to God, choosing to turn life's hardships into stepping stones for success. Pressing through an oppressive childhood, life-threatening abuse and sickness as an adult, Kathleen allows the Spirit of God to turn her tragedies into triumph and devastation into dedication. Victorious over her own hurtful situations, she now helps others discover truth to live a life of freedom.

A few of Kathleen's published works include the following: ...*In His Presence, Scripture Keys, His Heart Calls, Personal Poetic Promises from God's Word, The Truth about Lies* and *ABCs of Who I Am in Christ!* Her prolific skills in writing, proof-editing, design and typography help new and experienced authors publish books and quality products with a spirit of excellence. To learn more about Kathleen Schubitz or publishing and related services by RPJ & Company, visit RPJandco.com.

BOOKS BY KATHLEEN SCHUBITZ

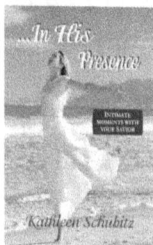

...In His Presence (Color)

Inspirational poetry and prose with full color images on every page. From the author's personal experiences come messages of love, comfort and healing for the soul. The poetry gently leads the reader into reflection and meditation.

Encouragement for every reader to pursue God, praising Him through all... whatever we choose to do ... let it be done in God's presence.

Paperback - ISBN: 978-0-9819980-1-5
Hardcover - ISBN: 978-1-937770-40-2

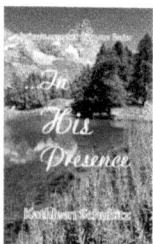

...In His Presence

In the revised and expanded edition, Kathleen offers more inspirational poetry and prose to encourage, uplift and edify God's children. The words come to life as they inspire each reader seeking answers through life's challenges. Each poem is accompanied by scripture for personal reflection along with a scriptural index for further study.

The first design is an entirely b/w book. The second design has a color cover with an acrostic on the back cover reading: Desire His Love.

Paperback - ISBN: 978-1-937770-42-6
Paperback - ISBN: 978-0-9819980-7-7

...In His Presence 40-Day Journal (Color)

Full color images with personalized verses on every page to make the experience of journaling a pleasurable and memorable one! Complete with a One-Year Daily Bible Reading Schedule.

Paperback - ISBN: 978-1-937770-44-0

BOOKS BY KATHLEEN SCHUBITZ

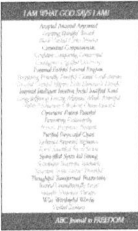

ABC Journal to Freedom
A companion book to the *ABC Woman Finds Freedom*.
It is designed to help people discover who they are in
Christ. Complete with two journal pages for each letter
of the alphabet; excluding the letter x.

Paperback - ISBN: 978-1-937770-62-4

ABC Woman Finds Freedom (Paperback)
A compilation of testimonies for women who find
themselves in a prison ... with or without bars! Women
whose lives were being lived in a prison of their own
minds found the simple lesson of changing the ABCs
and learning to think and agree with God's Word to
change their situations. Intended for prisoners and
prison ministry, anyone can change their thoughts and
words that ultimately lead to a life of freedom.

Paperback - ISBN: 978-1-937770-15-0
E-book - ISBN: 978-1-937770-14-3

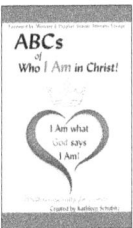

ABCs of Who I Am in Christ!
I Am What God Says I Am!
Verses to motivate, encourage and inspire the Christian
to walk in agreement with God's Word. More than
800 personal "I Am" statements for every day reading
or esteem-building. A little book with powerful truths!
Makes a great ministry tool for yourself or one to give
away! One version is for men and women; one version
created for women only.

(Women) Paperback - ISBN: 978-1-937770-29-7
(General) Paperback - ISBN: 978-1-937770-30-3

BOOKS BY KATHLEEN SCHUBITZ

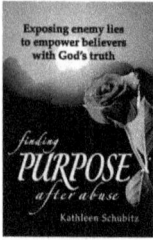

Finding Purpose after Abuse: Exposing enemy lies to empower believers with God's truth

The author motivates readers to pursue truth in relationships both with people and God. As her story unfolds, she inspires wounded hearts to seek healing from the Creator of the Universe. She reveals her need to re-learn and exchange lies once believed to be truth, and her need to lean on and trust a loving heavenly Father.

Leader's Guide - A companion to *Finding Purpose after Abuse*, intended for a 12-week Bible study course. Complete with questions and answers for assistance during the study.

ISBN: 978-1-937770-25-9
ISBN: 978-1-937770-51-8

God's New Wine

Inspired by a prophetic word to a local body of Christ, the message is for all believers. Designed with color and appeal on every page! Available in poster form, 16 x 12, laminated.

ISBN: 978-1-937770-60-0

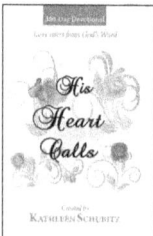

His Heart Calls: Love notes from God's Word

A daily devotional written in God's voice to draw the reader into His Word and promises to deepen the relationship with Him. For those seeking a deeper walk and trust with the Lord, it becomes active, powerful and life-changing to every soul searching for truth and intimacy. Designed with eye appeal for reading enjoyment. Personalized for every reader. It makes a great gift that will never expire!

KJV Paperback - ISBN: 978-1-937770-16-7
Color Hardcover - ISBN: 978-1-937770-41-9
Contemporary Paperback - ISBN: 978-1-937770-24-2

BOOKS BY KATHLEEN SCHUBITZ

Journal to Freedom (Color)
Updated interior with new cover design.
Every page is designed in full color with a peaceful sunset and red rose to draw one into the presence of the Lord. Meditating upon His Word and truth of who we are in Christ will allow the Holy Spirit to pour out through the heart onto each page.

ISBN: 978-0-9761122-6-6

Living With Purpose 30-Day Journal (Color)
Designed with full color images. Scripture verses included for reflection, quiet time and writing.

Paperback - ISBN: 978-1-937770-49-5

Lord, I Praise You...
Sowing seeds of gratitude
During times of worship with the Holy Spirit, *Lord, I Praise You* is designed as an interactive poetic devotional to help keep the believer focus on being grateful and thankful, despite life's challenges.

Paperback - ISBN: 978-1-937770-50-1

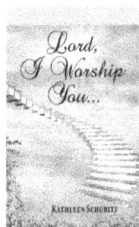

Lord, I Worship You...
During times of intimate worship with the Holy Spirit, *Lord, I Worship You* is a poetic devotional to draw the reader into a closer walk and relationship with Him.

Paperback - ISBN: 978-1-937770-38-9
Color Paperback - ISBN: 978-1-937770-37-2

BOOKS BY KATHLEEN SCHUBITZ

Personal Poetic Promises from God's Word

A devotional of personal promises (126) written in free style poetry form to encourage every reader any time of day. Designed with a flower border for reading enjoyment. Complete with scripture verses. A great gift for any occasion.

Paperback - ISBN: 978-1-937770-31-0
Color Paperback - ISBN: 978-1-937770-39-6

Personal Promises Journal

A journal book including promises (126) written in free style poetry form to encourage readers during quiet times and reflection. Complete with scripture verses and a Daily Reading Bible Schedule. It makes a great gift for any occasion.

Paperback - ISBN: 978-1-937770-57-0

Poetry: Healing for the soul (Vol 2)

Continuing the pursuit of truth and God's love, the poet shares her intimate moments of writing and inspiration. With a ready pen and heart, more verses are sure to touch the reader's heart. *Softcover. 32 pages*

ISBN: 978-1-937770-61-7

Scripture Keys: Inspiring words for your journey

A great gift idea. A pocket companion of nearly 900 scripture verses to encourage every reader in a daily walk and meditation time through God's word. Two designs available.

Color Paperback - ISBN: 978-1-937770-46-4
General audience - ISBN: 978-1-937770-34-1

BOOKS BY KATHLEEN SCHUBITZ

The Truth about Lies
Uncovering lies in a deceit-filled world

Do you feel overwhelmed by deceit, lies and deception all around? If too many poor choices led you into a dark dreary pit without a way of escape, there is hope. This book offers insight and solutions to open your eyes and ears to truth. Learn to walk free of lying spirits and subtle deception that surrounds our personal lives and floods our nation. Intended for spirit-filled believers, truth seekers and anyone who desires to be saved and live a spirit-filled life.

ISBN: 978-xxxxx

S.E.W. during a sunset or sunrise... Vol 1
Color Devotional/Journal

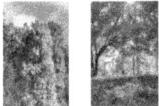

Designed with full color images. Encouraging words written to inspire people to grow and mature naturally as well as spiritually in God's Kingdom. Perfect for the busy individual who still desires a quick word during quiet times and reflection.

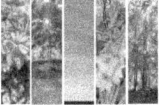

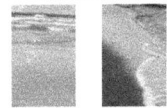

S.E.W. among the trees... Vol 2
Color Devotional/Journal

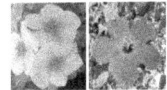

S.E.W. at the beach... Vol 3
Color Devotional/Journal

S.E.W. among the flowers... Vol 4
Color Devotional/Journal

SCAN THE CODE TO SEE MORE BOOKS

www.ingramcontent.com/pod-product-compliance
Lightning Source LLC
Chambersburg PA
CBHW021123020426
42331CB00004B/598